KING JAMES VERSION

Holy Bible

Coloring Book

Psalms, Scripture & Bible Verses

VOLUME I

First edition published 2023
© Illumina Books 2023
Cover artwork and original illustrations by Illumina Books
Descriptions by Olivia Goodhope
Contact: illuminacoloringbooks@gmail.com

Thank you for your purchase!

Information on this title: amazon.com/author/illuminabooks

Shop our other books at Illumina Books: amazon.com/author/illuminabooks

Questions and customer service: email us at: illuminacoloringbooks@gmail.com

Sharing is caring! Join our online community https://www.instagram.com/iluminabooks

Books from the 'KJV Bible Verses Coloring Book' Series	Publishing Details
KJV Holy Bible Illustrated Kids Coloring Book - Psalms, Scripture & Bible Verses (Volume 1)	ISBN: 9-798868-436338
KJV Holy Bible Illustrated Kids Coloring Book - Psalms, Scripture & Bible Verses (Volume 2)	ISBN: 9-798868-436734
KJV Holy Bible Illustrated Kids Coloring Book - Psalms, Scripture & Bible Verses (Volume 3)	ISBN: 9-798868-441547

Other Titles by Illumina Books (Español)

RVA Santa Biblia Ilustrado Libro de colorear para niños - Salmos, Escrituras & Versículos (Volumen 1)	ISBN: 9-798871-306390
RVA Santa Biblia Ilustrado Libro de colorear para niños - Salmos, Escrituras & Versículos (Volumen 2)	ISBN: 9-798871-306840
RVA Santa Biblia Ilustrado Libro de colorear para niños - Salmos, Escrituras & Versículos (Volumen 3)	ISBN: 9-798871-307281

Dedicated to Grandma, whose faith and love of coloring books always inspires me.

Exclusively distributed and printed by Amazon, Inc., its affiliates, distribution partners and/or subsidiaries.

Printed on black ink on 74-90 GSM white paper: suitable for pencil , charcoal or pastels; ink or markers may bleed.

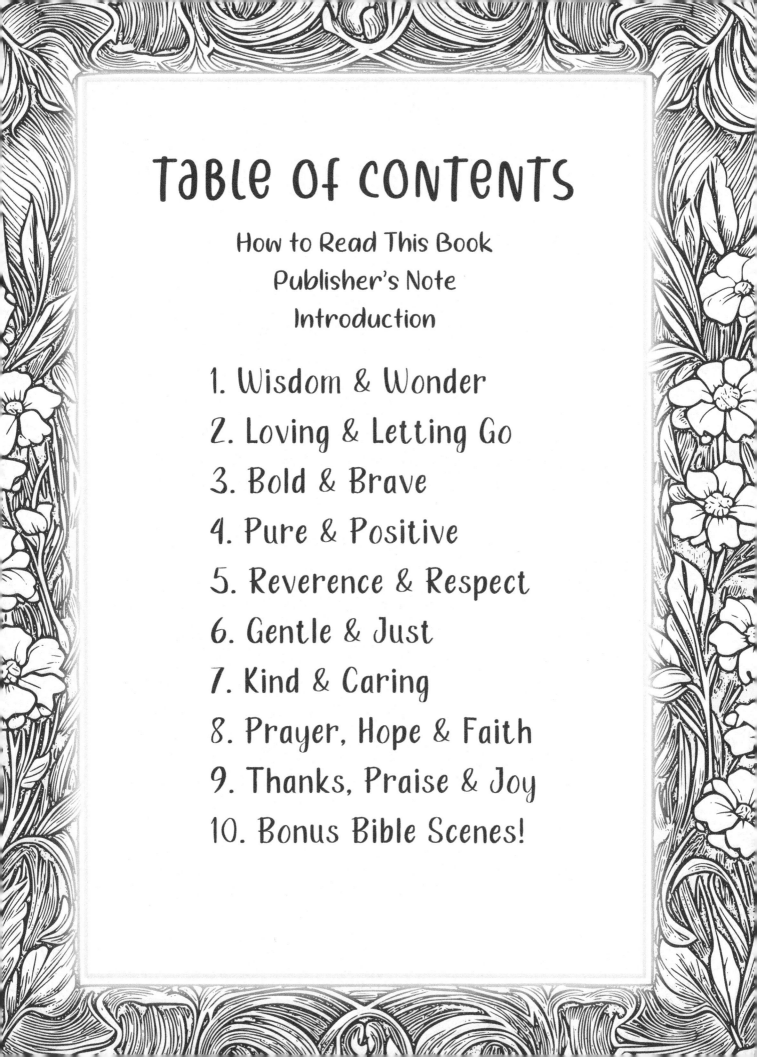

Table of Contents

How to Read This Book
Publisher's Note
Introduction

collect the whole series!

King James Version – Holy Bible (English)

Reina–Valera Antigua – Santa Biblia (Español)

I have called thee by thy name

Isaiah 43:1

_____

Insta: @illuminabooks

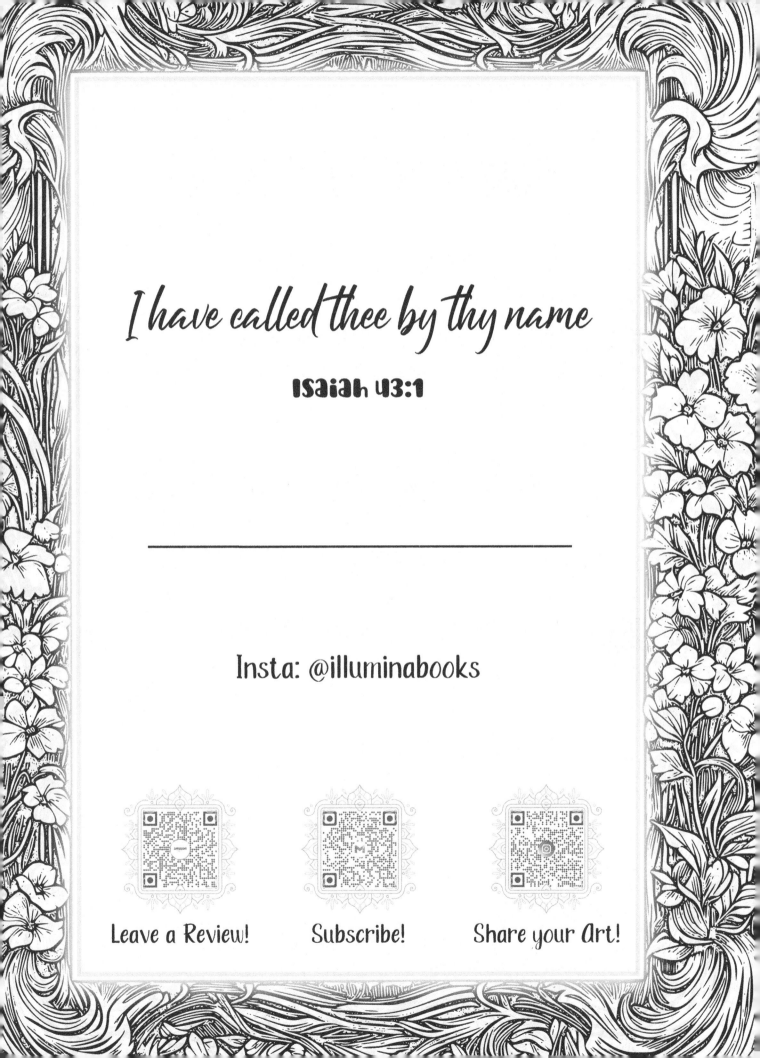

Leave a Review!   Subscribe!   Share your Art!

How to Read this Book

This is an interactive coloring book!

With your parent's permission, scan each QR Codes using the camera on your Smart Phone or Tablet!

Each QR Code link provides you with free and instant access to the full KJV verse, similar KJV verses and an online KJV Dictionary!

Try it below to reveal a bonus KJV Bible verse!

KJV Verse   KJV Dictionary   Similar Verses

PUBLISHER'S NOTE

Dear parents,

Thanks for choosing Illumina Books! We're a small team of artists and religious scholars dedicated to creating books that will ignite your child's imagination and deepen their connection with God.

The King James Version of the Holy Bible has inspired countless millions, offering profound wisdom and divine truth as a timeless companion for daily prayer.

Our interactive coloring books series aims to be a fun and meaningful resource for your child's bible study for years to come. For questions or comments, please reach out to us at illuminacoloringbooks@gmail.com.

Yours faithfully,
Illumina Books

ILLUMINA BOOKS

INTRODUCTION

Hey Kids!

Explore the 1st book in our 3 part "KJV Holy Bible Kids Coloring Book" series with illustrated psalms, scriptures, and bible verses to color in from all 66 main books of the KJV Holy Bible!

Each saying is organized into helpful chapters, arranged by topic and the order they appear in the KJV. QR Code links to full quotations and similar KJV verses are available wherever we've shortened text.

Fun fact: Did you know the KJV was first published in 1611? That's over 400 years ago! If you find the language a bit out of date, simply scan the QR Code link to access a helpful online KJV dictionary!

Discover a fun and illuminating way to engage in your bible study with Illumina Books. Happy coloring!

CHAPTER 1

WISDOM & WONDER

"In the beginning, God created the heavens and the earth"

Genesis 1:3

KJV Verse　　　KJV Dictonary　　　Similar Verses

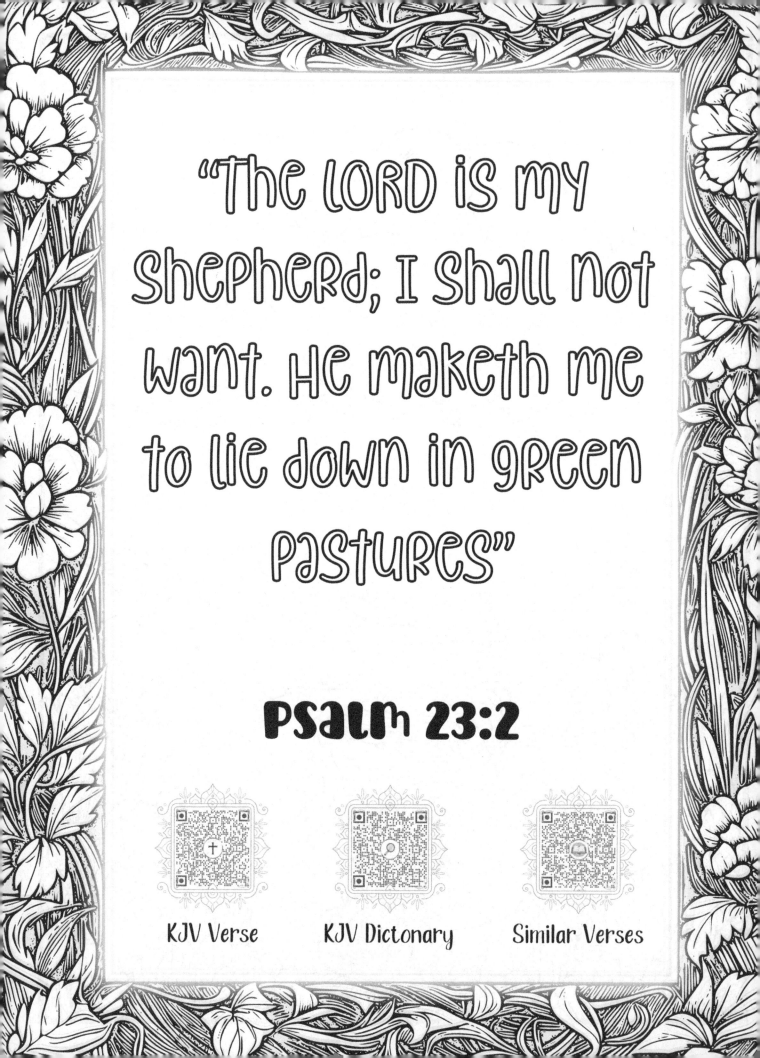

"The LORD is my shepherd; I shall not want. He maketh me to lie down in green pastures"

PSALM 23:2

KJV Verse   KJV Dictonary   Similar Verses

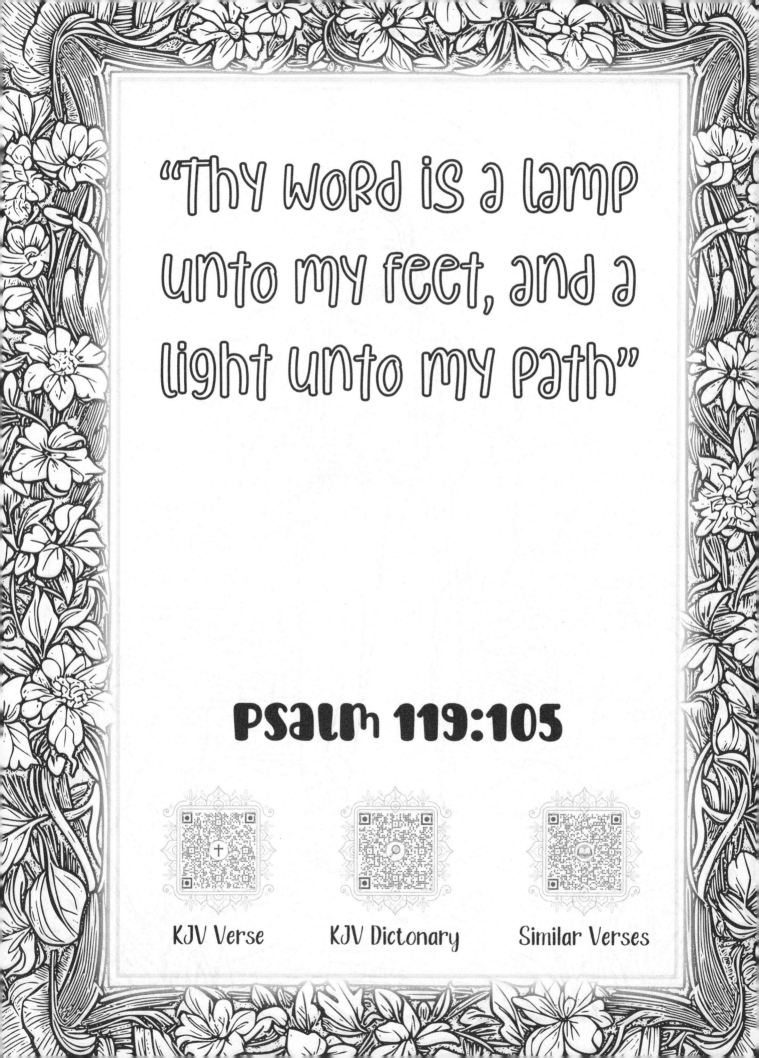

"Thy word is a lamp unto my feet, and a light unto my path"

PSALM 119:105

KJV Verse

KJV Dictonary

Similar Verses

"The fear of the LORD is the beginning of wisdom"

Proverbs 9:10

KJV Verse · KJV Dictonary · Similar Verses

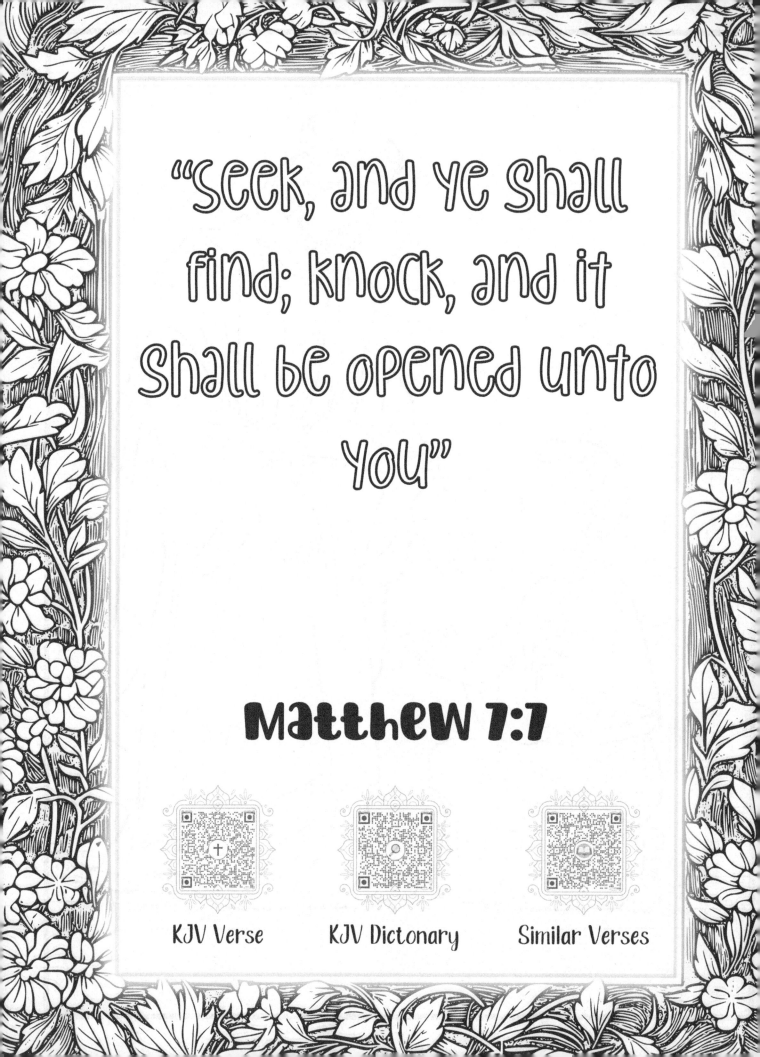

"Seek, and ye shall find; knock, and it shall be opened unto you"

MATTHEW 7:7

KJV Verse   KJV Dictonary   Similar Verses

"Whatsoever a man soweth, that shall he also reap"

Galatians 6:7

KJV Verse

KJV Dictonary

Similar Verses

CHAPTER 2

LOVING & LETTING GO

"Love the LORD thy GOD with all thine heart, and with all thy soul, and with all thy might"

Deuteronomy 6:5

KJV Verse

KJV Dictonary

Similar Verses

"love your enemies, bless them that curse you, do good to them that hate you"

Matthew 5:44

KJV Verse

KJV Dictonary

Similar Verses

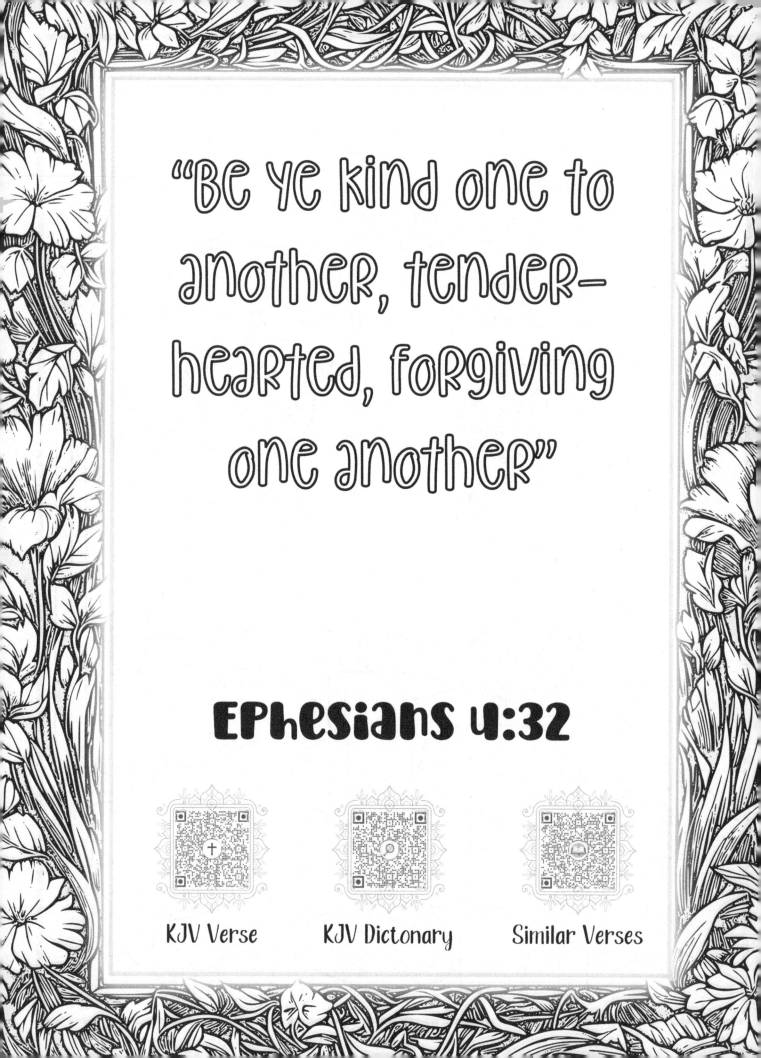

"Be ye kind one to another, tender-hearted, forgiving one another"

EPHESIANS 4:32

KJV Verse

KJV Dictonary

Similar Verses

"Love one another, as he gave us commandment"

1 John 3:23

KJV Verse   KJV Dictonary   Similar Verses

"He that loveth not knoweth not GOD; for GOD is love"

1 John 4:8

KJV Verse   KJV Dictonary   Similar Verses

"GOD is love; and he that dwelleth in love dwelleth in GOD, and GOD in him"

1 John 4:16

KJV Verse   KJV Dictonary   Similar Verses

"We love him, because he first loved us"

1 John 4:19

KJV Verse KJV Dictonary Similar Verses

CHAPTER 3

BOLD & BRAVE

"Be strong and of a good courage... for the LORD thy GOD is with thee"

JOSHUA 1:9

KJV Verse   KJV Dictonary   Similar Verses

"The LORD is my light and my salvation; whom shall I fear?"

PSALMS 27:1

KJV Verse   KJV Dictonary   Similar Verses

"The LORD is my strength and my shield"

PSALM 28:7

KJV Verse   KJV Dictonary   Similar Verses

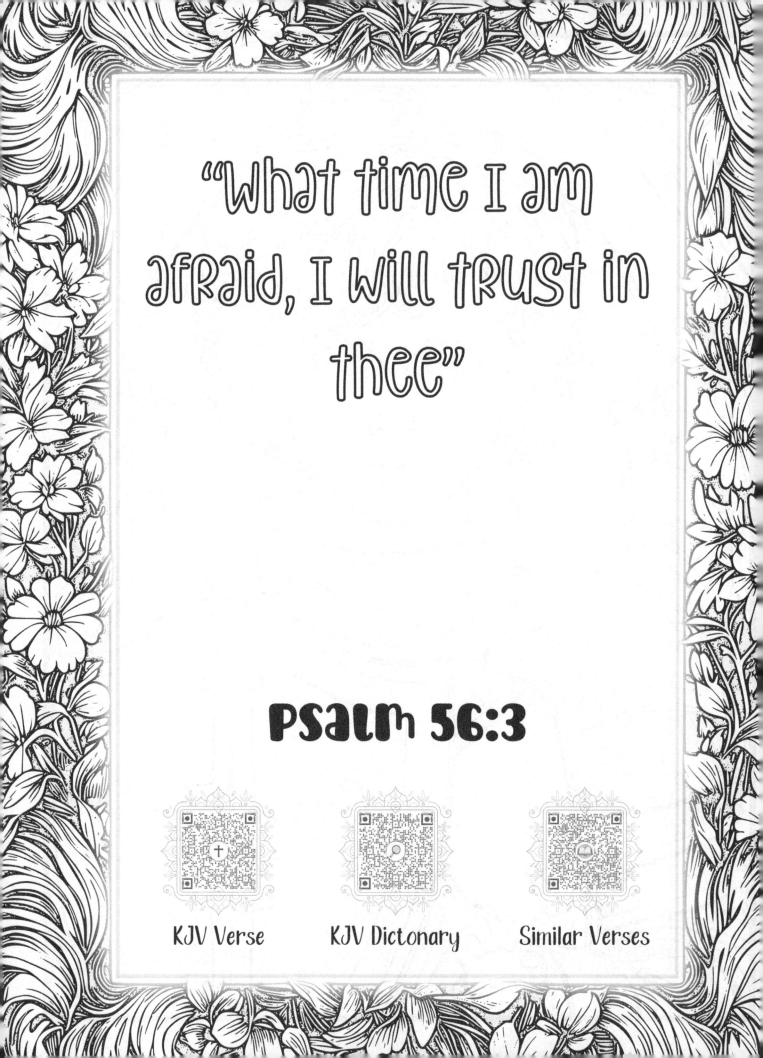

"What time I am afraid, I will trust in thee"

PSALM 56:3

KJV Verse KJV Dictonary Similar Verses

"Be not overcome of evil, but overcome evil with good"

ROMANS 12:21

KJV Verse   KJV Dictonary   Similar Verses

"I can do all things through christ which strengtheneth me"

PHILIPPIANS 4:13

KJV Verse   KJV Dictonary   Similar Verses

CHAPTER 4

PURE & POSITIVE

"a wise son maketh a glad father"

Proverbs 10:1

KJV Verse   KJV Dictonary   Similar Verses

"a child is known by his doings, whether his work be pure, and whether it be right"

proverbs 20:11

KJV Verse   KJV Dictonary   Similar Verses

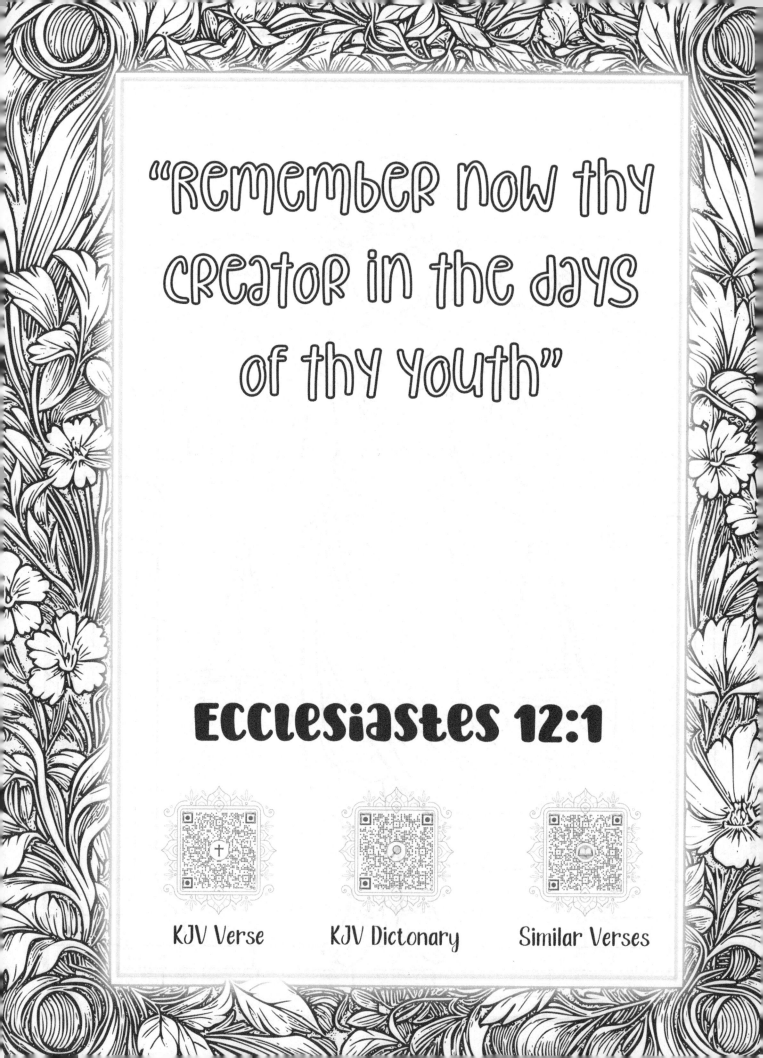

"Blessed are the pure in heart: for they shall see GOD"

MATTHEW 5:8

KJV Verse   KJV Dictonary   Similar Verses

"Whosoever shall not receive the kingdom of GOD as a little child, he shall not enter therein"

Mark 10:15

KJV Verse   KJV Dictonary   Similar Verses

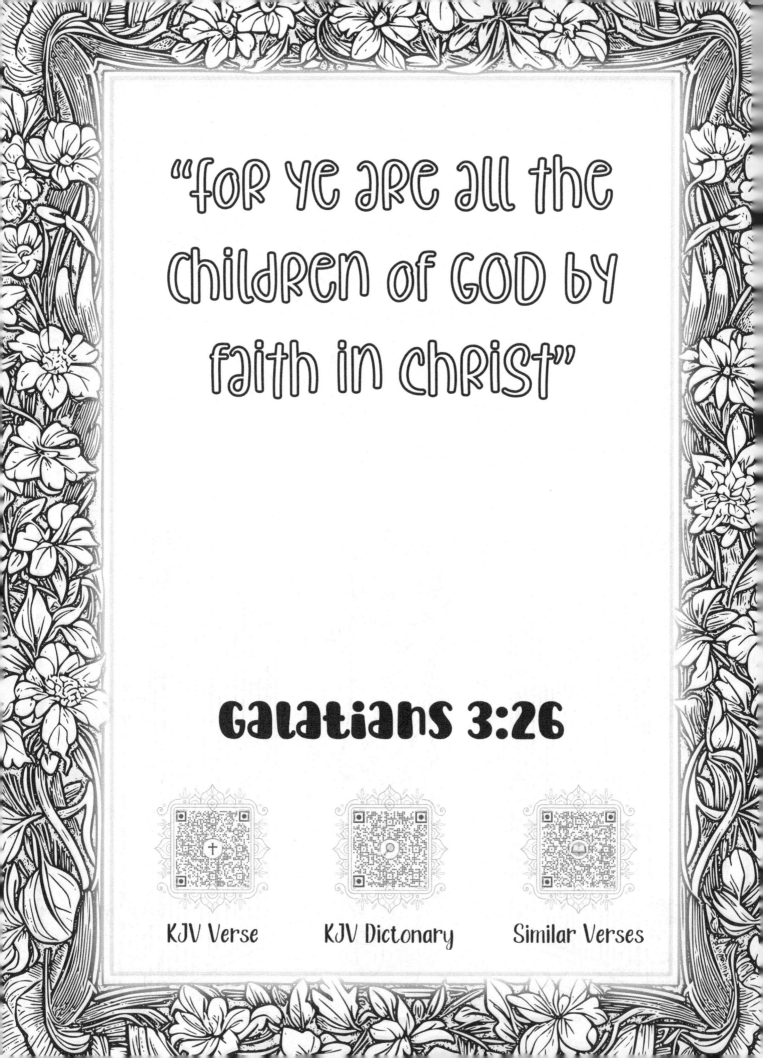

"for ye are all the children of GOD by faith in Christ"

GALATIANS 3:26

KJV Verse

KJV Dictonary

Similar Verses

"Be ye therefore followers of GOD, as dear children"

EPHESIANS 5:1

KJV Verse   KJV Dictonary   Similar Verses

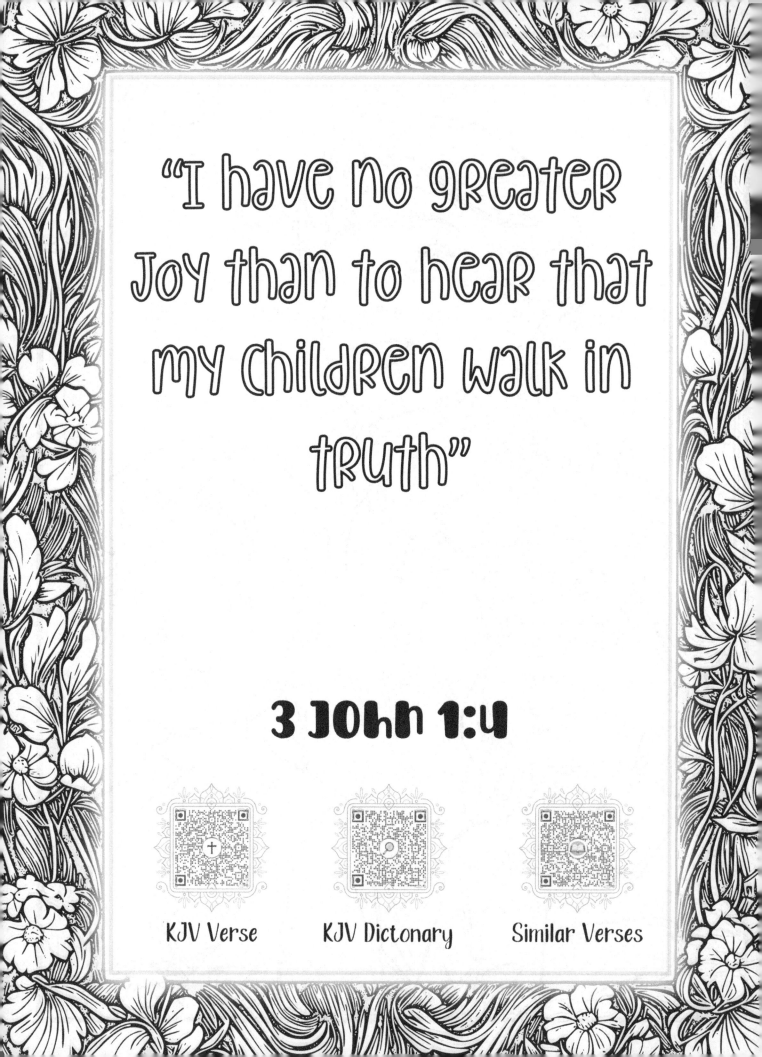

"I have no greater joy than to hear that my children walk in truth"

3 John 1:4

KJV Verse

KJV Dictonary

Similar Verses

CHAPTER 5

RESPECT & REVERENCE

"Honour thy father and thy mother: that thy days may be long upon the land"

EXODUS 20:12

KJV Verse   KJV Dictonary   Similar Verses

"Train up a child in the way he should go: and when he is old, he will not depart from it"

Proverbs 22:6

KJV Verse   KJV Dictionary   Similar Verses

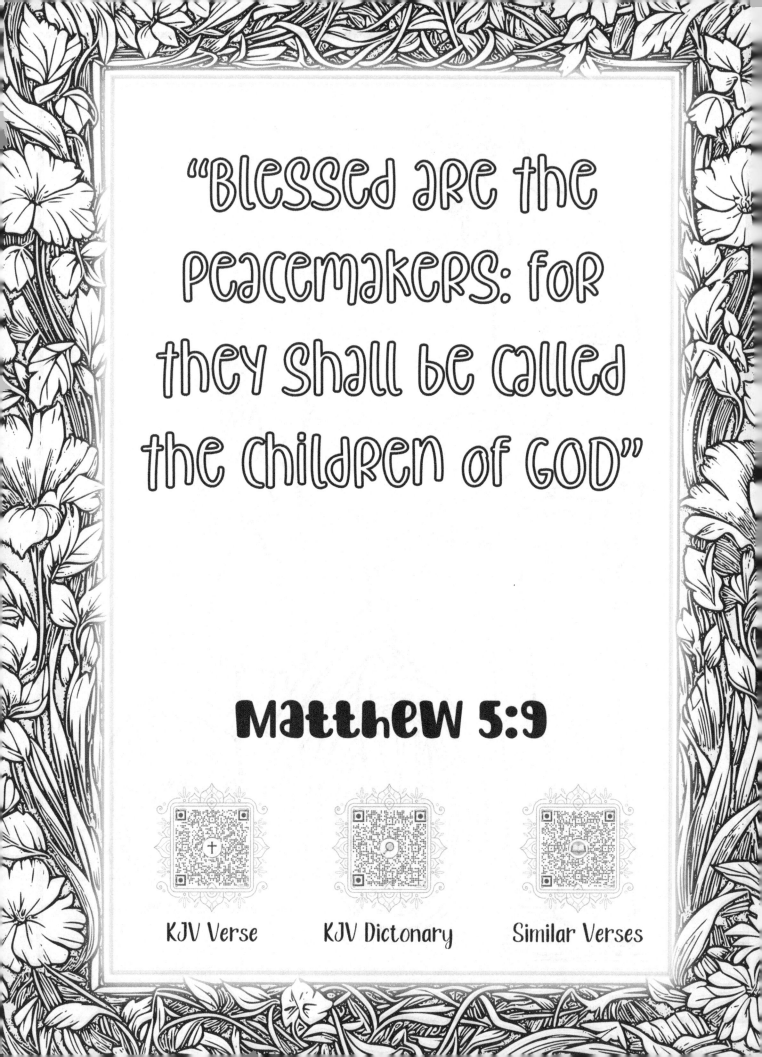

"Blessed are the peacemakers: for they shall be called the children of GOD"

MATTHEW 5:9

KJV Verse   KJV Dictonary   Similar Verses

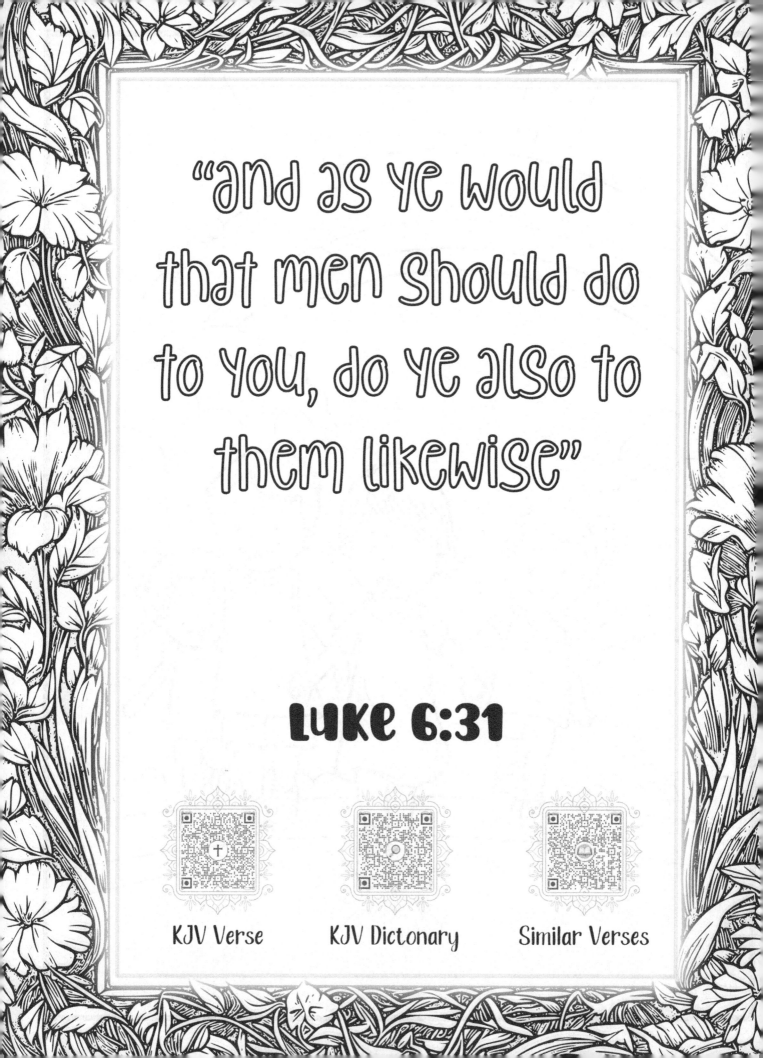

"And as ye would that men should do to you, do ye also to them likewise"

LUKE 6:31

KJV Verse   KJV Dictonary   Similar Verses

"Children, obey your parents in the LORD: for this is right"

EPHESIANS 6:1

KJV Verse

KJV Dictonary

Similar Verses

CHAPTER 6

GENTLE & JUST

"Take heed what ye do: for ye judge not for man, but for the LORD"

2 CHRONICLES 19:6

KJV Verse   KJV Dictonary   Similar Verses

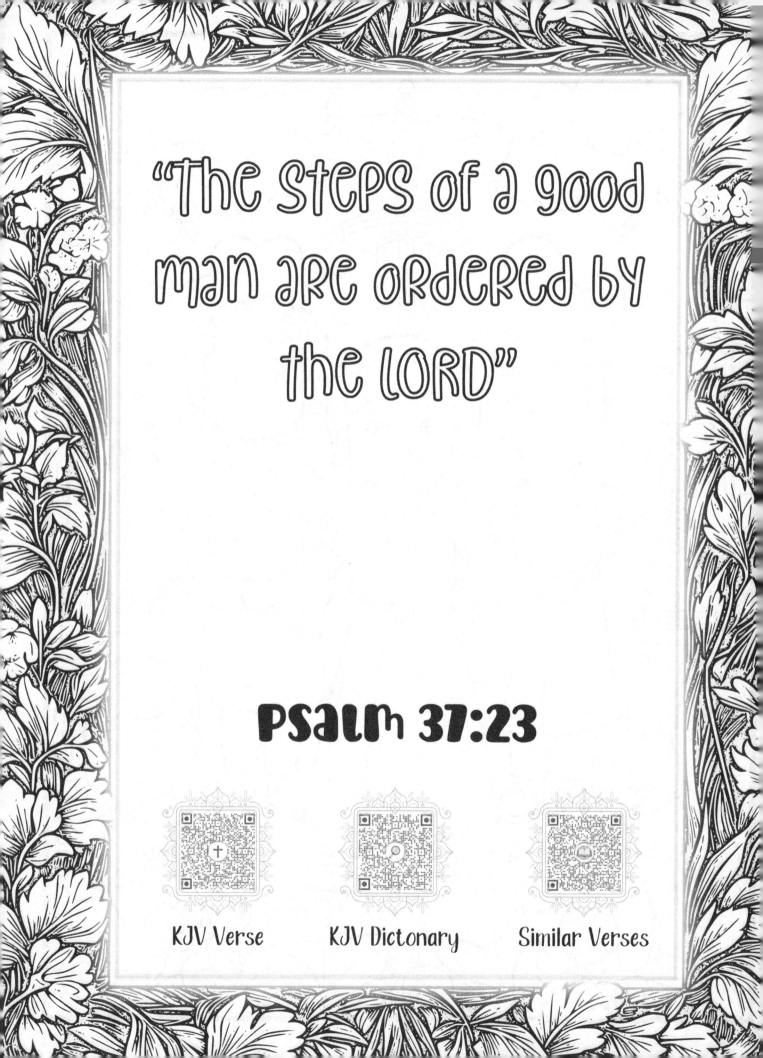

"The steps of a good man are ordered by the LORD"

PSALM 37:23

KJV Verse   KJV Dictonary   Similar Verses

"The path of the just is as the shining light"

Proverbs 4:18

KJV Verse

KJV Dictonary

Similar Verses

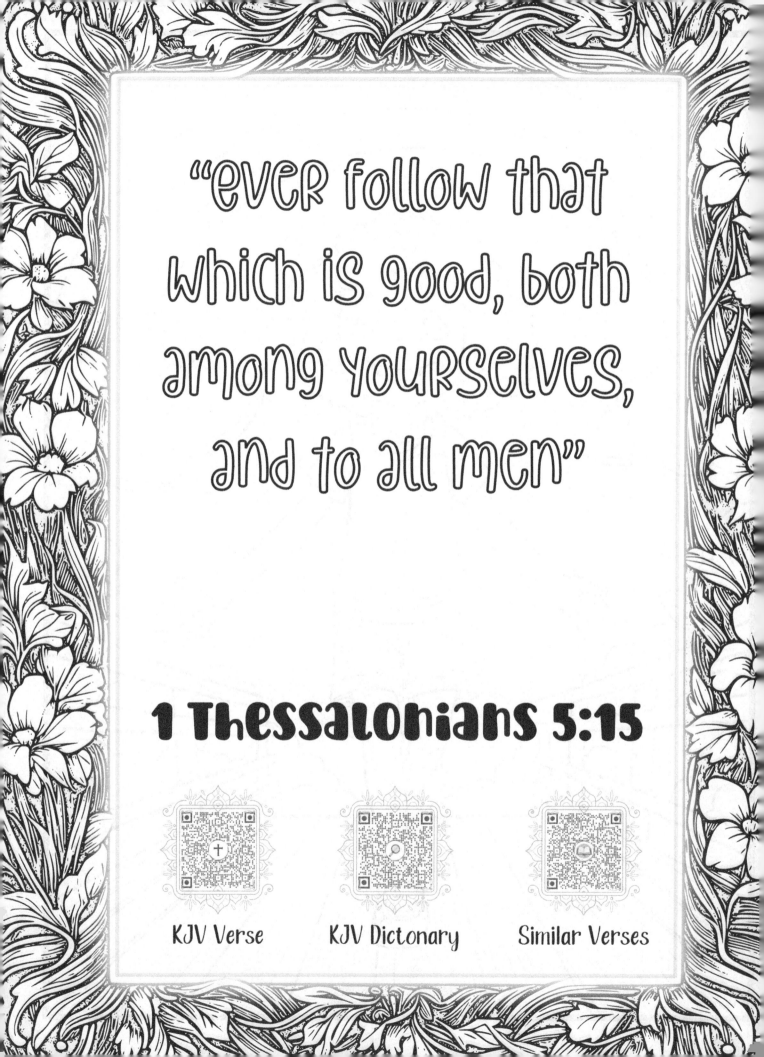

"ever follow that which is good, both among yourselves, and to all men"

1 Thessalonians 5:15

KJV Verse   KJV Dictionary   Similar Verses

"Be ye doers of the word, and not hearers only"

JAMES 1:22

KJV Verse

KJV Dictonary

Similar Verses

CHAPTER 7

KIND & CARING

"charity never faileth"

1 Corinthians 13:8

KJV Verse   KJV Dictonary   Similar Verses

"faith, hope, charity...
the greatest of
these is charity"

1 Corinthians 13:13

KJV Verse   KJV Dictonary   Similar Verses

"let all your things be done with charity"

1 corinthians 16:14

KJV Verse   KJV Dictonary   Similar Verses

CHAPTER 8

PRAYER, HOPE & FAITH

"TRUST in the LORD
with all thine heart"

Proverbs 3:5

KJV Verse KJV Dictonary Similar Verses

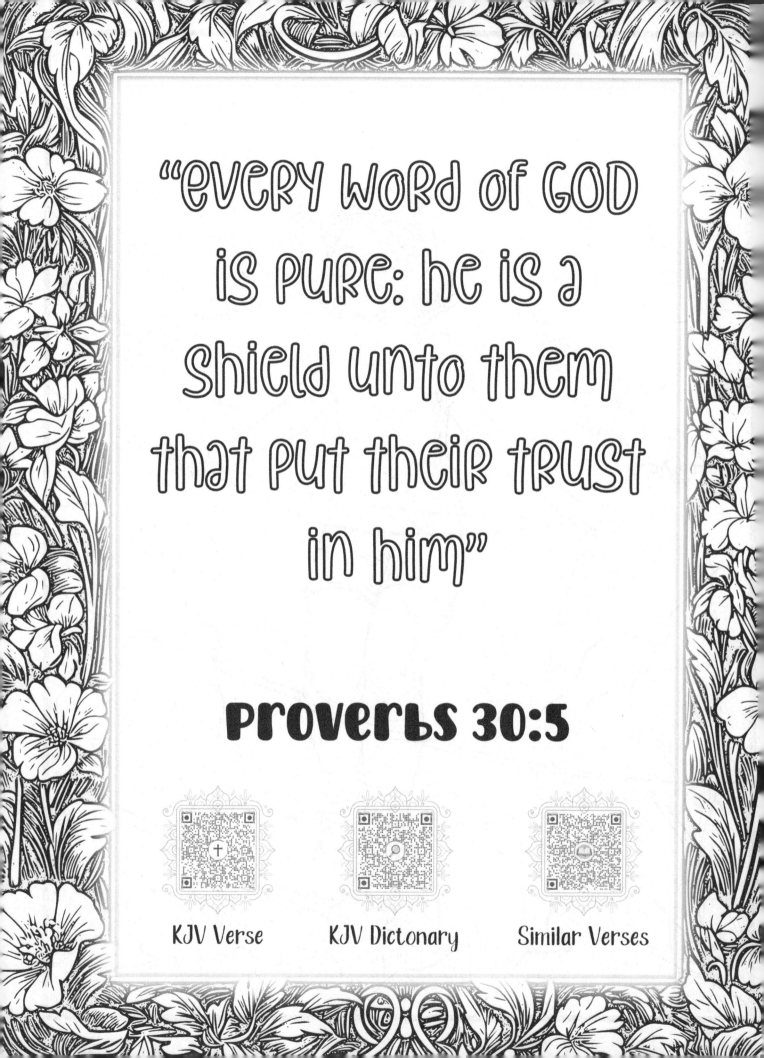

"every word of GOD is pure: he is a shield unto them that put their trust in him"

Proverbs 30:5

KJV Verse   KJV Dictonary   Similar Verses

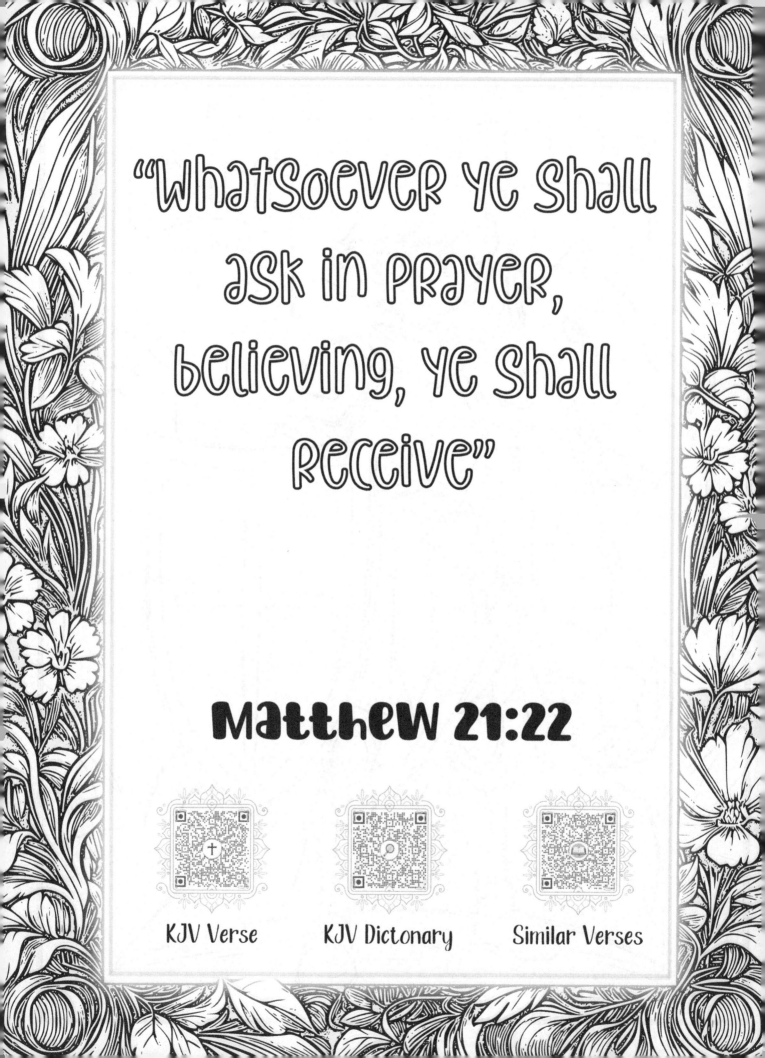

"Whatsoever ye shall ask in prayer, believing, ye shall receive"

Matthew 21:22

KJV Verse   KJV Dictonary   Similar Verses

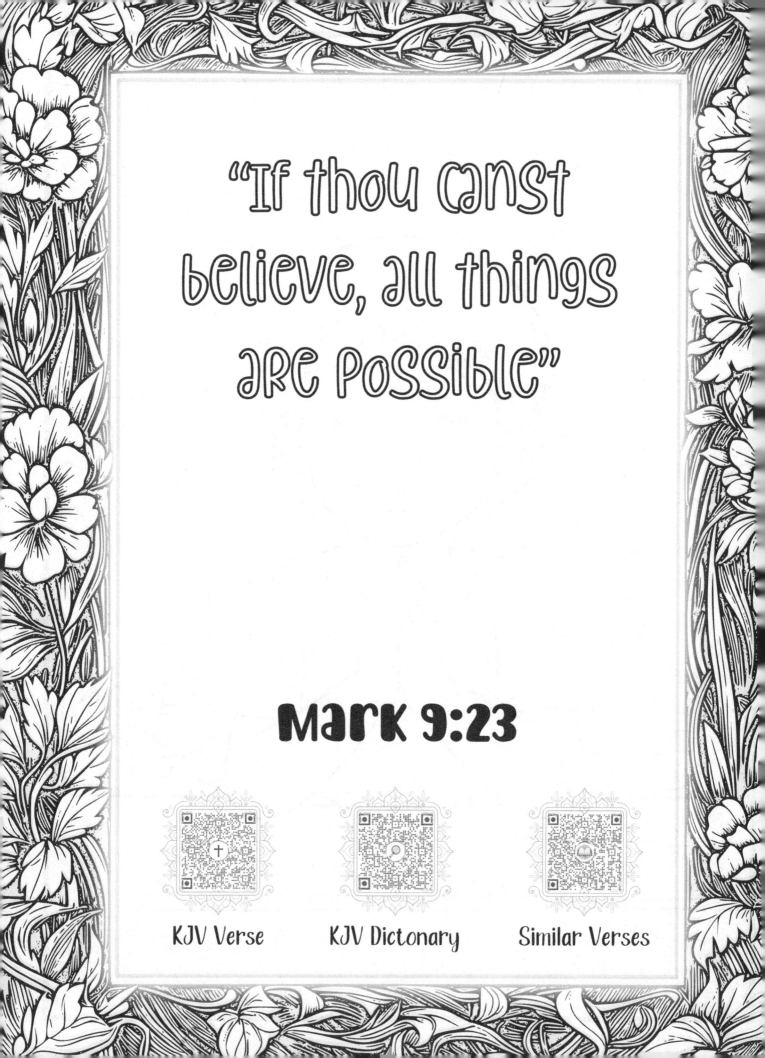

"If thou canst believe, all things are possible"

MARK 9:23

KJV Verse   KJV Dictonary   Similar Verses

"for we walk by faith, not by sight"

2 corinthians 5:7

KJV Verse

KJV Dictonary

Similar Verses

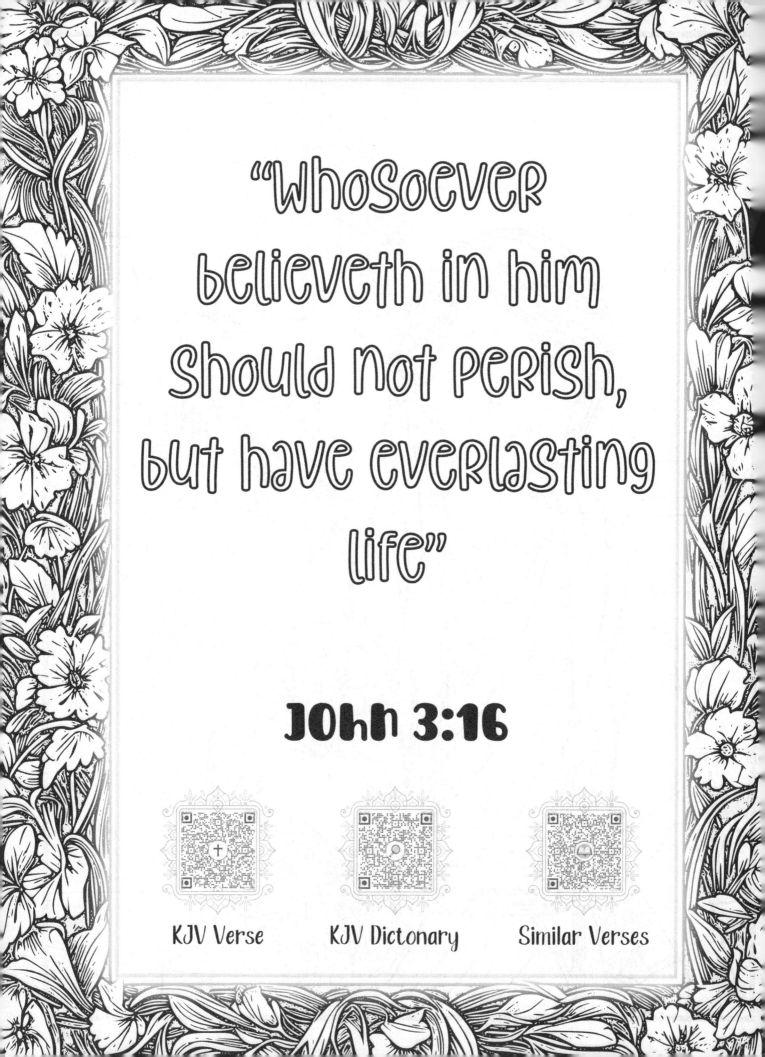

"Whosoever believeth in him should not perish, but have everlasting life"

John 3:16

KJV Verse   KJV Dictionary   Similar Verses

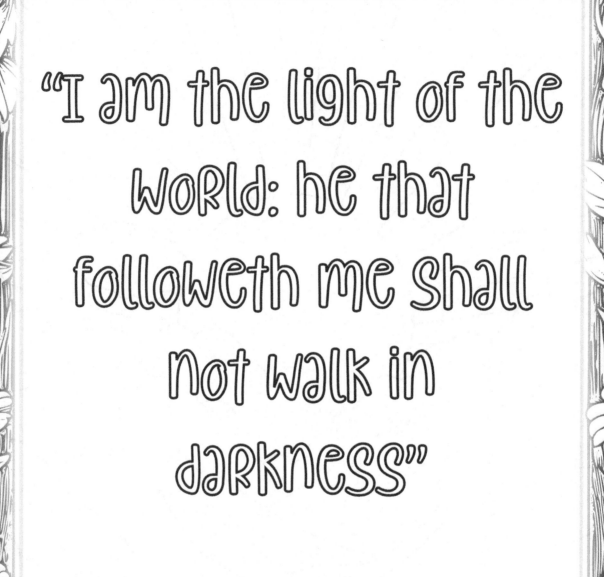

"I am the light of the world: he that followeth me shall not walk in darkness"

JOhn 8:12

KJV Verse

KJV Dictonary

Similar Verses

"I am the way, the truth, and the life"

JOHN 14:6

KJV Verse | KJV Dictonary | Similar Verses

CHAPTER 9

THANKS, PRAISE & JOY

"I will praise thee; for I am fearfully and wonderfully made"

PSALMS 139:14

KJV Verse   KJV Dictonary   Similar Verses

"The LORD is good to all"

PSALM 145:9

KJV Verse   KJV Dictonary   Similar Verses

"I am the LORD, I change not"

MALACHI 3:6

KJV Verse   KJV Dictonary   Similar Verses

"The fruit of the spirit is love, joy, peace, longsuffering, gentleness, goodness, faith..."

Galatians 5:22

KJV Verse   KJV Dictonary   Similar Verses

"Jesus christ the same yesterday, and to day, and for ever"

Hebrews 13:8

KJV Verse

KJV Dictonary

Similar Verses

"GOD is light, and in him is no darkness at all"

1 John 1:5

KJV Verse   KJV Dictonary   Similar Verses

"I am the vine, ye are the branches"

John 15:5

KJV Verse

KJV Dictonary

Similar Verses

CHAPTER 10

BONUS BIBLE SCENES!

"and the LORD GOD formed man of the dust of the ground"

GeneSiS 2:7

KJV Verse   KJV Dictonary   Similar Verses

"Make thee an ark of gopher wood"

Genesis 6:14

KJV Verse   KJV Dictonary   Similar Verses

"Let my people go, that they may serve me"

EXODUS 8:1

KJV Verse　　　KJV Dictonary　　　Similar Verses

"for the battle is the LORD'S"

1 Samuel 17:47

KJV Verse   KJV Dictonary   Similar Verses

"I am the good shepherd: the good shepherd giveth his life for the sheep"

John 10:11

KJV Verse   KJV Dictonary   Similar Verses

Join the fun!

Leave a Review!

Share Your Art!

Subscribe to our Newsletter!

Collect the Whole Series!

Well done!

""Well done, thou good and faithful servant"! (Matthew 25:21). Congratulations on finishing this Illumina Coloring Book!

We hoped you enjoyed each of these 60 coloring pages and found the Psalms, Scriptures and Bible Verses to be full of faithful inspiration!

As the Holy Bible says, "charity never faileth" (1 Corinthians 13:8) ! If you liked this book, please use the QR Codes on the left to buy others in the series, leave a review on Amazon, subscribe to our newsletter or (with your parent's permission) share your art with us on Instagram @illuminabooks!

Until our next coloring adventure, as the hymnist Sabine Baring-Gould says, "Onward, Christian soldiers!" Happy coloring!